yukismart.com/b/6a0a58
AF365373
1
2

մեկ

mek

pineapple

արքայախնձոր

ark ayaxnjor

guitar

կիթառ

kit a

2

two

երկու
erkow

dinosaurs

դինոզավրեր
dinozavrer

twins

երկվորյակներ
erkvoryakner

3

three

երեք
erek

starfishes

ծովաստղեր
covastłer

peaches

դեղձեր
dełjer

4

four

շորս
č ors

cherries

բալեր
baler

robots

ոոբոսներ
obotner

5

five

Հինգ
hing

fingers

մատներ
matner

pencils

մատիտներ
matitner

6

six

վեց
vec

candies

կոնֆետներ
konfetner

hearts

սրտեր
srter

7

seven

յոթ
yot

seashells

ծովախեցգիներ
covaxec iner

blocks

խորանարդիկներ
blokner

8

ants

մրջյուններ

mrǰyownner

flowers

ծաղիկներ

cał̇ikner

9

fishes

ձկներ

jkner

buttons

կոճակներ

kočakner

10

ten

տասը

tasə

candles

մոմեր

momer

eggs

ձվեր

jver

2 4 6 8 10

even

 նույնիսկ

nowynisk

1 3 5 7 9

odd

կենտ

tarōrinak

whole

ամբողջ
ambołǰ

half

կես
kes

red

կարմիր
karmir

umbrella

հովանոց
hovanoc

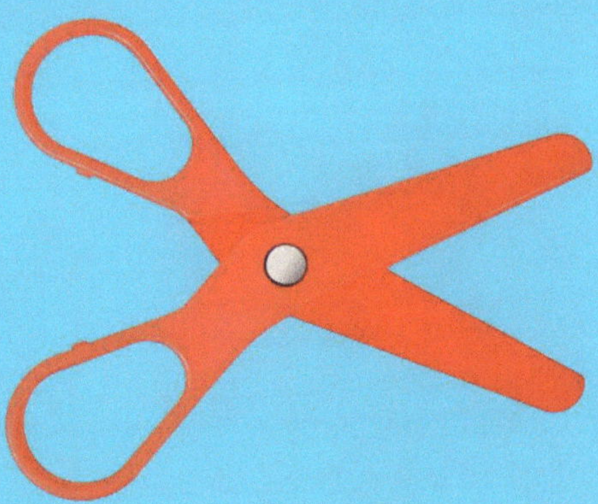

scissors

մկրատ
mkrat

yellow

դեղին
dełin

banana

բանան
banan

cheese

պանիր
panir

green

կանաչ

kanač

vegetables

բանջարեղեն

banǰarełen

bottle

շիշ

šiš

gray

մոխրագույն

moxragowyn

carpet

գորգ

gorg

feather

փետուր

p etowr

orange

նարնջագույն

narnǰagowyn

pumpkin

դդում

ddowm

orange juice

նարնջի հյութ

narnǰi hyowt

white

 սպիտակ

spitak

cup

բաժակ

bažak

envelope

ծրար

crar

black

սև

sEV

glasses

ակնոց

aknoc

shirt

վերնաշապիկ

vernašapik

brown

շագանակագույն

šaganakagowyn

violin

ջութակ

ǰowt ak

cake

տորթ

t xvack

blue

կապույտ

kapowyt

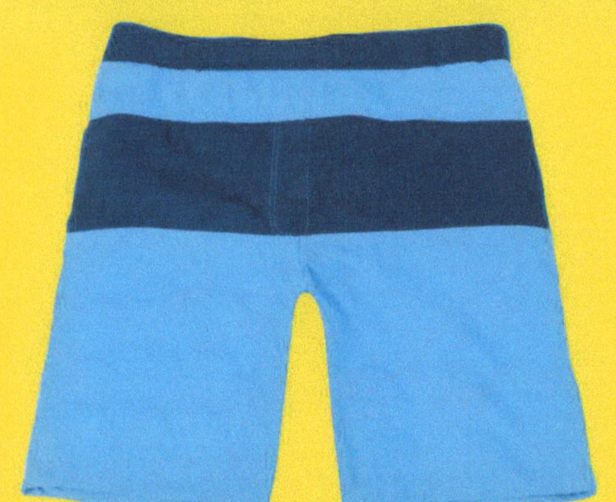

swim shorts

լողալու շորտ

lołalow šort

swimming goggles

լողի ակնոցներ

lołi aknoc ner

pink

վարդագույն

vardagowyn

ice cream

պաղպաղակ

pałpałak

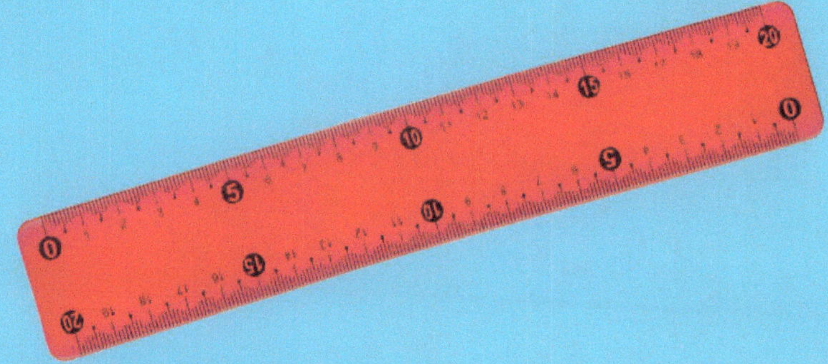

ruler

քանոն

k anon

purple

մանուշակագույն

manowšakagowyn

dice

զառեր

za er

fan

հովհար

hovhar

light colors

բաց գույներ
bac   gowyner

dark colors

մուգ գույներ
mowg gowyner

circle

շրջան

šrǰan

square

քառակուսի

k a akowsi

star

աստղ

astł

heart

սիրտ

sirt

crescent

կիսալուսին
kisalowsin

triangle

եռանկյուն
e ankyown

rectangle

ուղղանկյուն
owłłankyown

oval

ձվածիր
jvacir

drop

կաթիլ

kat il

cross

խաչ

xač

cube

խորանարդ

xoranard

sphere

գունդ

gownd

ring

օղակ

ōłak

trefoil

երեքնուկ

erek nowk

cylinder

գլան

glan

cone

կոն

kon

line

line

զիծ

gic

arrow

arrow

սլաք

slak

dots

dots

կետեր

keter

zigzag

զիգզագ

zigzag

curve

կոր

kor

spiral

պարուրաձև

parowrajew

draw

Նկարել

nkarel

paint

Ներկել

nkarel

count

Հաշվել

hašvel

write

գրել

grel

small

փոքր

p ok r

big

մեծ

mec

mouse

մուկ

mowk

elephant

փիղ

p ił

short

կարճ

karč

long

երկար

erkar

worm

որդ

ord

snake

օձ

ōj

thin

բարակ
barak

thick

հաստ
hast

empty

դատարկ
datark

full

լի
li

1
2
3

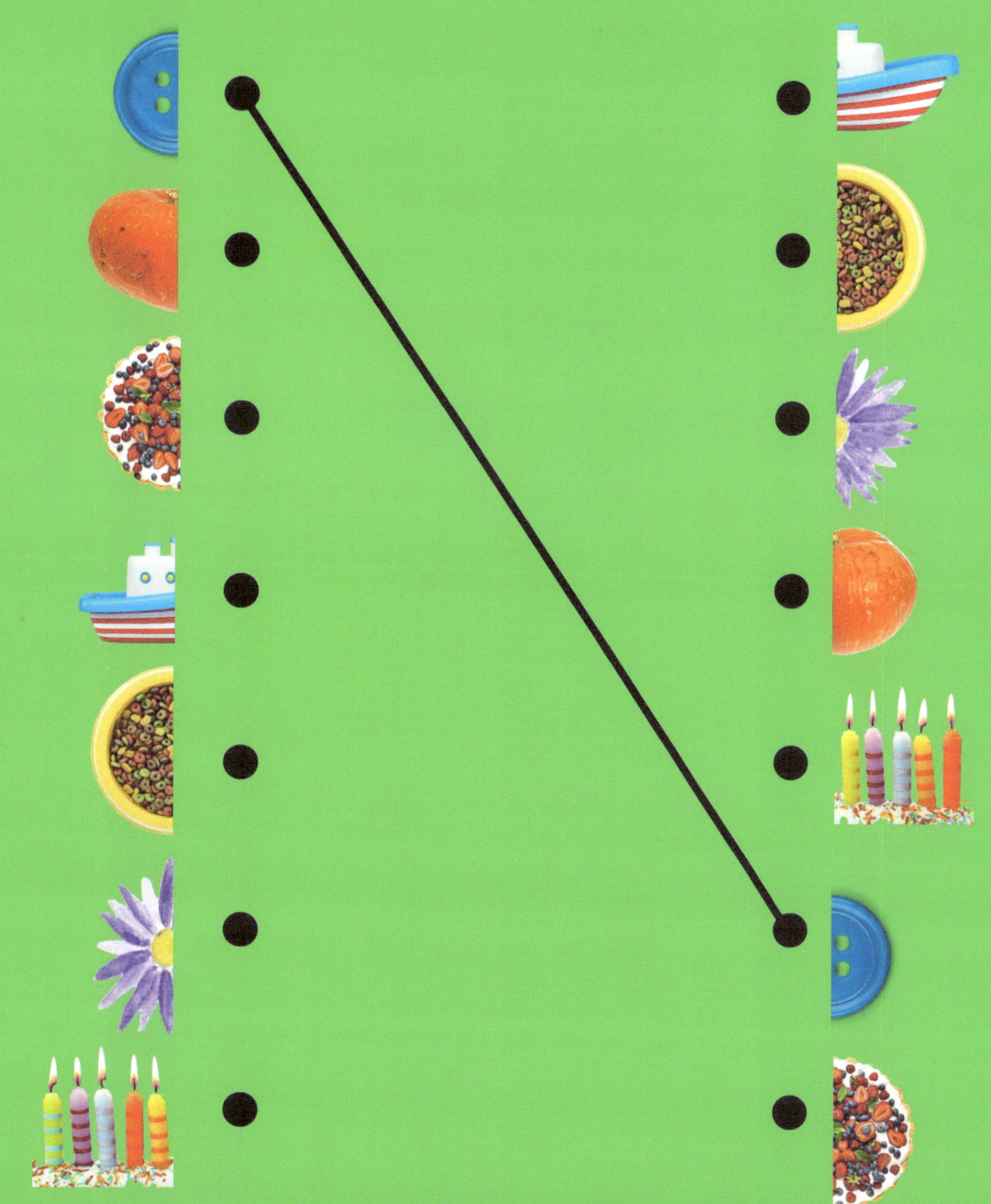